THE · MACDONALD · ENCYCLOPEDIA · OF

Mammals

Luigi Boitani
and Stefania Bartoli

Macdonald

Edited by Sydney Anderson

The publishers would like to thank the following Australian institutions for their assistance: Adelaide Zoo; the Cleland Conservation Park, Starling; Victor Harbor's Urimbissa Fauna Park; Melbourne Zoo; the Sir Colin Mackenzie Fauna Park, Healesville; the Taronga Zoo, Sydney; the Western Plains Zoo, Dubbo; the Tidbindilla Nature Reserve (Australian Capital Territory); the Lone Pine Koala Sanctuary, Brisbane; and Mr S. J. Cowling of the Fisheries and Wildlife Division, Melbourne. Our thanks are also extended to the Rice Creek Biological Field Station (USA).

A **Macdonald** BOOK

© 1982 Arnoldo Mondadori Editore S.p.A., Milan
© 1983 in the English translation
    Arnoldo Mondadori Editore S.p.A., Milan

Translated by Simon Pleasance

First published in Great Britain in 1986
by Macdonald & Co (Publishers) Ltd
London & Sydney

A member of BPCC plc

British Library Cataloguing in Publication Data

Macdonald encyclopedia of mammals.
    1. Mammals — Dictionaries
    I. Anderson, Sydney
    599'.003'21   QL701.2

    ISBN 0-356-12422-3

Printed and bound in Italy
by Officine Grafiche A. Mondadori Editore, Verona

Macdonald & Co (Publishers) Ltd
Greater London House
Hampstead Road
London NW1 7QX

THE · MACDONALD · ENCYCLOPEDIA · OF

Mammals

CONTENTS

KEY TO SYMBOLS

Habitat   Though many species occupy two or more types of habitat in nature, the usual or preferred habitat of each species is shown by one of the following symbols:

desert

grassland, plain,
prairie, steppe, scrub

savanna

evergreen broadleaf
woodland

deciduous forest

coniferous forest

tundra and ice

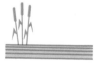

swamp, marshland

tropical or
subtropical forest

rivers and lakes,
estuaries

seas and oceans

high rocky slopes,
upland meadows

Maps indicate approximate distribution of species within their appropriate habitats.

Color of map indicates abundance or rarity of each species, based upon the *Red Data Book* of the International Union for the Conservation of Nature and other current literature, and is shown as follows:

Red: threatened with extinction

White: rare

Yellow: endangered

Green: common or not endangered

Gray: status underdetermined

NOTES ON SPECIES ENTRIES

The scientific, or Latin, name is stated for each species, followed by common or vernacular name(s) most often used.
Classification indicates the order and family of each species and follows the taxonomy usually employed today. Variations in nomenclature are given for clarity in certain cases.
Description generally refers to average-size specimens, except where a range of measurements is given or records of exceptional specimens are noted.
Distribution supplements that shown on the map and applies to the entire species.
Habitat is described for each species in more detail than can be indicated by the symbol.
Behavior covers habits, reproduction, economic importance, or other data on the natural history of each species.
Notes of general interest are sometimes included.

THE VARIETY OF MAMMALS

Mammals are the most diversified of all creatures living on earth today. They range from minute shrews to gigantic whales. The blue whale is the largest living mammal; a species of tiny bat from Thailand is the smallest. In addition, the variety of shapes, coloration, and behavioral patterns of mammals is greater than in most other animal classes. Mammals have colonized every environment. They have mastered the techniques of swimming and burrowing, and have achieved true flight. They live in equatorial and polar regions alike, and feed on whatever food resources are available. There is no doubt that they have taken on a predominant role. Perhaps surprisingly, there are not many mammals—approximately 4,000 species, compared with about 7,500 species of reptiles and amphibians or 8,600 species of birds. Mammals represent a very advanced stage in the long process of animal evolution: the complexity—physiological and behavioral—of an organism such as a mammal is unmatched by that of any other animal. Over relatively short periods of geologic time, when compared with the long periods needed by other animal classes, mammals have assumed widely varied ecological roles, taking over from more ancient forms of animal life.

We ourselves—that is, mankind (*Homo sapiens*)—are also mammals and naturally share with other mammalian families our complex anatomy and physiology, as well as much in our behavioral patterns. And precisely because of his natural affinity with other mammals, man has selected from them those animals which are now his closest companions, such as the domestic dog and cat. A variety of species have taught us about ourselves through observation and scientific experimentation. Man has also destroyed countless fellow mammals under the banner of "sport." And finally, mammals have found themselves burdened with the task of providing man with his major food resources. Human progress has often been at the expense of our fellow mammals. It is thus quite natural that we should have a special regard for these creatures.

Many mammals are not readily seen in the daytime, nor are they easy to observe and study. A number of species are known only from specimens lodged in museum cabinets; we have no knowledge of their lives. Many mammals have only a neutral coloration, and so fail to attract the notice of laymen. The result is that most of us are acquainted only with the striking or sensational species, and it is left to the specialists to fill in the gaps in our information bank. Before we discuss the structure of a mammal and its classification, let us first see how these animals came into being.

THE ORIGIN AND EVOLUTION OF MAMMALS

The origin of the first mammals dates back to evolutionary efforts made by certain reptiles about 250 million years ago. Mammals, like birds, owe their presence on earth to the remarkable range of forms that reptiles displayed for literally

Mammals display a wide versatility, and have adapted to virtually all habitats on land and in the sea.

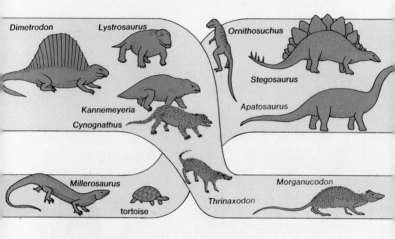

millions of years. The Permian period began 270 to 280 million years ago. It was to last for 45 to 55 million years and was characterized by upheavals in the earth's crust, glaciations, and cold, wet climates. The earth's land was still in the form of two large continents, Laurasia in the Northern Hemisphere (including North America and Eurasia without peninsular India) and Gondwanaland in the Southern Hemisphere (combining South America, Africa, peninsular India, Antarctica, Australia, and New Zealand). During this period there was a proliferation of the most varied forms of insects, and this was possibly to have a decisive effect on the structure of the first mammals. In fact, the Permian period saw the first development of characteristics that later became mammalian. These were in the synapsids, or "mammal-like" reptiles. The most plausible theory today maintains that such small and medium-sized reptiles evolved certain characteristics which enabled them to occupy a new and rich ecological niche, revolving around the exploitation of those new and plentiful insects and of small nocturnal vertebrates, which hid by day from the large predatory reptiles. One of these reptiles evolving in the direction of mammals was *Dimetrodon*. This creature, whose fossil remains are found in Texas, was about 10 feet long and weighed almost 550 pounds. Like other reptiles, it was ectothermic—that is, its body temperature depended on heat absorbed from the surrounding environment. Its activity was thus closely linked with the outside temperature. *Dimetrodon* had an enormous sail-like crest on its back, extending from head to tail. This crest

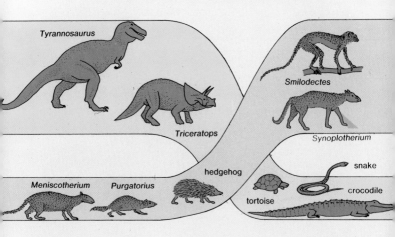

may have enabled it to absorb heat rapidly and thereby raise its own body temperature in a much shorter time than that required by other reptiles. In addition, by means of a mechanism to control its peripheral circulation, *Dimetrodon* might delay dissipation of the heat accumulated. Thus we see the first step toward the evolution of homeothermy, or the ability to maintain a constant body temperature.

Other synapsid reptiles of small and medium size evolved toward forms more closely resembling mammals. Compared with the large carnivorous reptiles, their small size helped them considerably because they could warm themselves up in a shorter time. They, too, fed on insects. There was then a transition from the Synapsida to more specialized forms known as the Therapsida. These advanced mammal-like reptiles, such as *Cynognathus*, a dog-sized predatory carnivore with teeth quite akin to those of true mammals, and the probably herbivorous *Kannemeyeria*, with a beaklike proboscis, appeared in the early part of the Triassic period, some 220 million years ago. Their gait was more mammalian than reptilian. They could move along swiftly on their four legs with their body raised above the ground. But the Triassic was also the period when other reptiles enjoyed an unequaled evolutionary gain. This was the birth of the Age of Dinosaurs. As large dinosaurs multiplied, almost all the synapsids and therapsids disappeared, with the exception of just a few survivors that were gradually evolving toward the first true mammals.

During the Jurassic period, 190 to 136 million years ago, with

Dimetrodon, *a mammal-like reptile, had a large crest on its back, which may have helped the animal to absorb or dissipate heat and thereby partially control its own body temperature.*

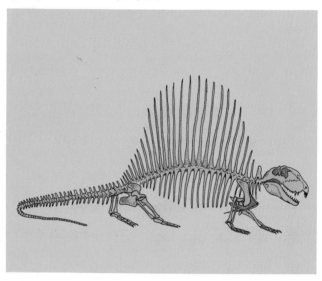

the reign of the mighty dinosaurs, early mammals had to be content with crumbs when it came to sharing the earth's resources. Thus they stayed in the form of small nocturnal animals with little ecological significance. The dinosaurs and great flying pterosaurs continued to dominate throughout the Jurassic and the Cretaceous period that followed, 136 to 65 million years ago. But by the mid-Cretaceous, the archaic mammals had split into two distinct groups. These were the marsupials, primitive relatives of today's North American opossum, and the placentals, which in their earliest forms were similar to modern shrews and hedgehogs. Toward the end of the Cretaceous the evolution of mammals got a boost in preparation for that veritable explosion of different forms which marks the following period. The Cretaceous saw the appearance of *Purgatorius*, a very ancient primate that lived in North America and resembled present-day tree shrews.

Some 65 million years ago saw the opening of the Tertiary period. Almost all the large reptiles which had ruled the world for more than 100 million years became extinct. In a relatively short time the earth's fauna underwent radical changes. We do not know why the dinosaurs became extinct; the currently favored hypothesis is based on the notion of far-reaching climatic changes which these specialized reptiles could not long endure. We call the Tertiary the Age of Mammals, for it was they who then dominated while the remaining reptiles were relegated to a secondary role. The well-adapted homeothermic mammals, with their high mobility, more complex brain, and

In (1) reptiles the mandible, or lower jaw, is articulated with the cranium by means of two bones, the quadrate and the articular, whereas in (2) mammals these two small bones have shifted inside the middle ear to form the incus and the stapes (or stirrup bone), which, together with the malleus, direct the vibrations of the tympanum (the eardrum) to the inner ear.

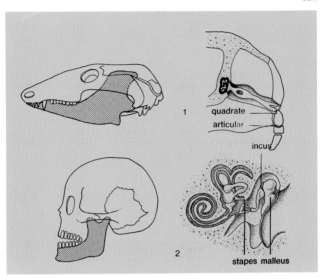

efficient system of rearing their young, had definite advantages when it came to filling the vacancies left by the great reptiles. The Tertiary is divided into seven epochs, corresponding to phases in the evolution of the mammal fauna and marked by different climatic and geologic events.

The first epoch, the Paleocene, lasted from 65 to 53 million years ago, when tropical and temperate climates became widespread and thus prepared the environment for new animal forms. The most primitive ungulates—browsing herbivores—appeared then. These condylarths, such as *Meniscotherium*, became common. They gave rise to a wide variety of hoofed mammals. Other Paleocene mammals remained substantially the same as those of the Cretaceous period; the few innovations included primitive armadillos in South America and the earliest tree-dwelling primates.

From 53 to 37 million years ago the Eocene epoch saw the globe somewhat as it is today. The vast northern and southern land masses had already broken up. North and South America were separated from one another as were Europe, Africa, and Asia; Australia and Antarctica were also separate continents. Although there were glaciers in some montane regions, such as western North America, tropical and temperate conditions prevailed as in the Paleocene. Besides marsupials, almost all the principal orders of land-dwelling placental mammals had now made their appearance. A group known as the Creodonta flourished. They were rat-size to dog-size carnivorous creatures, somewhat squat, with heavy limbs, and gave rise to the vast array of today's carnivores. Whales also appeared in the Eocene, represented by *Zeuglodon,* 60 feet in length with a very long tail. Among the land-dwelling creatures was *Uintatherium,* so called because its fossil remains were first found in the Uinta mountains of Utah. This grotesque animal, as large as a rhinoceros, bore six horns on its elongated head, had two stout tusks, and was herbivorous. The forerunners of rhinos, tapirs, pigs, and cattle also arose in the Eocene, as did the ancestors of the elephants, then trunkless, which originated in Africa. This period likewise saw the arrival of the first precursor of the horse. This was *Hyracotherium,* or eohippus, the "dawn horse," which had four toes on its front feet and three on its hind feet, and was the size of a small dog. An Eocene skeleton of *Icaronycteris,* the oldest known bat, was found in Wyoming. Primitive primates——ancestors of the monkeys and apes yet to evolve——were widespread. These small, agile creatures gave rise to arboreal lemurs, lorises, and tarsiers. As we draw closer to present times and enter the Oligocene, 37 to 26 million years ago, we find many Eocene mammals being replaced by the ancestors of modern forms. Bats became diversified; elephants, still small, developed short trunks and bore four tusks. The little "dawn horse" was succeeded by its slightly larger descendant *Mesohippus.* The giant, hornless rhinoceros, *Baluchitherium,* lived in Asia during the Oligocene. It was the largest land mammal ever known, standing 16 to 18 feet high at the shoulders, and probably ate leaves. Even-toed ungulates, herbivorous animals having a pair of toes on each foot, became abundant. They included primitive camels in North America, ancestral deer, and many piglike and hippolike forms. Carnivores such as the forerunners of modern dogs, cats, bears, and the hyena preyed upon the Oligocene fauna; many of the prey doubtless were rodents and rabbits, similar to their present-day descendants.

The Age of Mammals reached its zenith in the Miocene epoch, 26 to 5 million years ago. It was a time of geologic and climatic upheaval, when the massive Himalayan and Alpine ranges were formed and the continents assumed dimensions similar to those of today. Tropical climates gave way to temperate, resulting in vast dry grasslands, or prairies, and even deserts. Great herds of herbivores spread through the woods and plains. There were now different sorts of horses, and there were rhinoceroses, giraffes, the first deer to wear antlers, giant pigs, cattle, camels, and antelopes displaying three or four horns, often in weird shapes. Elephants evolved into several types, had grown in size, and with many other species invaded new lands at a time when Europe was joined with Asia as well as with North Africa and North America, as a result of both land movements and changes in ocean depth. Just as the immense grasslands provided sustenance for the numerous species of grazing mammals, so too those creatures were themselves a food source for many carnivores——ancestral dogs, civet cats, bears and others. Foremost among them were small but effective sabertooth cats.

Diverse species of mammals declined during the subsequent Pliocene (5 to 1.8 million years ago) and Pleistocene (1.8 mil-

In the Cretaceous period, when mammals were beginning to develop, marsupials and placentals split into separate groups. The murine opossum (Marmosa) and the white-toothed shrew (Crocidura) are present-day examples of these groups.

lion to 10 thousand years ago) epochs. Primates, however, continued their adaptive radiation. It was in east Africa that the primates displayed those most interesting modifications that led to the first humans. Possibly the first creature leading directly to man was *Ramapithecus,* a Miocene ape that died out in Asia but survived in Africa. And it is the appearance of these primates that marked the beginning of the decline of mammals and ushered in the Pleistocene, in which we see the rise of man and the disappearance of many mammal species. These extinctions were caused mainly by the very harsh glacial conditions which four times prevailed over the northern third of the earth's surface. The last glaciation began to retreat northward about 10,000 years ago——at the close of the Pleistocene——and is still retreating. Only those species which could adapt to such a climate managed to survive——as did, for example, the woolly mammoth with its shaggy coat and heavy layer of fat. During the Pleistocene, however, mammalian evolution no longer continued in the direction of sophisticated specialization of different species, as had occurred in the Miocene, but rather pushed toward a smaller number of species that could adapt more satisfactorily to a changing environment——in other words, less specialized species. The birth and rise of man is the best example of this new strategy of adaptation. It was only in Africa that mammals continued to live as they had done for millions of years, and in fact the present-day African savanna is a typical Miocene setting. From ancient *Ramapithecus* and perhaps Pleistocene *Australopithecus,* via *Homo erectus*——who lived from 1.5 million to 300,000 years ago——we ultimately emerged as *Homo sapiens* some 100,000 years ago.

DISTRIBUTION

The mammals we see today, and *where* we find them, are results of a complicated process involving the formation and extinction of species, movements and migrations, and competition and balance between species. It is mandatory that a species disperse if it is to survive. Young animals move away from the home territory of their parents and establish their own home range in an area that may satisfy their needs. Such a move could be a few feet; it could be miles. The pressure of increasing populations forces a species to spread over ever-widening areas, so that in time it may occupy an entire region and have adapted to a variety of living conditions, or produced descendant species that have so adapted.

The capability for such dispersal depends upon a number of factors. Large, highly mobile mammals and those that fly can disperse over a greater distance than burrowers. The animals' tolerance for different environmental conditions is also important. If a prairie dweller, for example, can exist in wooded country, it may disperse farther from its origin than a species that cannot survive outside the grasslands. And finally, natural barriers impede dispersal. Such barriers may be rivers, lakes or seas, mountain ranges, different climates, or zones of different vegetation.

North America and Eurasia appear to be major centers where certain families of mammals originated; other families first appear in South America and Africa. Migrations of species must have occurred, and such movements could take place only when and where natural routes existed. A considerable exchange of fauna between Asia and Europe could be expected when the two continents were joined; a significant, though lesser, exchange would occur across land bridges only occasionally connecting continents, as between Siberia and Alaska; and very few land mammals would make it across an ocean to populate islands, perhaps by means of floating debris. For example, one species of bat was the only land mammal to reach Hawaii without the intervention of man.

Thus geologic changes and the dispersal process have contributed to the evolution of species and helped create today's picture of the earth's fauna. To put it simply, the fauna of each region in the world consists of descendant species whose ancestors came to the area in different periods, by different means, and from various regions.

The modern science concerned with the distribution of animal life is zoogeography. One of the cornerstones in this field was laid just over a century ago by the great English naturalist Alfred Russel Wallace, the codiscoverer, with Charles Darwin, of the principle of natural selection. In what Wallace himself considered his "most important scientific work," he delineated the six faunal realms into which the earth could be divided. Zoogeographers still use Wallace's divisions, which are:

Ethiopian Region. Embraces southern Arabia, Madagascar, and Africa north to the Atlas Mountains, but excluding the coastal strip north of the Sahara.

Oriental Region. Includes tropical Asia—that is, India, Indochina and southern China, Malaya, the Philippines, and Indonesia east to an imaginary line approximately between Borneo and Celebes, and between Java and Lombok.

Palearctic Region. Made up of Africa north of the Sahara and the whole of Eurasia, except the Indian subcontinent and southeast Asia.

Nearctic Region. Constitutes the whole of North America north of the tropics in Mexico.

Neotropical Region. Embraces all the New World southward from tropical Mexico.

Australian Region. Includes Australia with Tasmania, New Guinea, Celebes, and the small islands of Indonesia east of Borneo.

When taken together, the Nearctic and Palearctic are termed the *Holarctic Region.* The world's oceans can be taken as an added *Oceanic Region.* There are no native land mammals inhabiting Antarctica.

The Ethiopian Region is joined to the Palearctic by Egypt and the Sinai Peninsula. It is composed of the most varied environments, from deserts to tropical forests, tundra to savanna. Because of this variety of habitats the fauna is also diversified. No fewer than 14 families of mammals are endemic to this region. Nearly all the genera of antelope are too. Two genera of great apes—the gorilla and the chimpanzee—are African, as is the

The zoogeographical regions

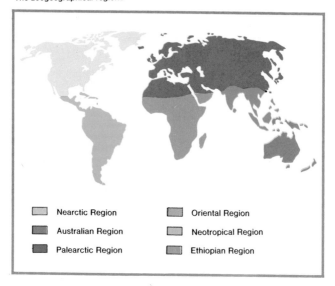

Nearctic Region

Oriental Region

Australian Region

Neotropical Region

Palearctic Region

Ethiopian Region

array of Old World monkeys. This region also includes the peculiar fauna of Madagascar, with lemurs being the most spectacular example of endemism, or the occurrence of an animal or plant in one area and nowhere else. The small viverrid carnivores (civets and mongooses) display their greatest variety of forms in the Ethiopian Region; 23 of the 25 genera are native.

The Oriental Region is characterized by tropical climates and forests. This region is separated from the Palearctic by deserts to the west and the Himalayan range to the north. The mammal fauna is similar to that of the Ethiopian Region, and in fact about 78% of the families are common to each. The presence in both these regions of rhinoceros, elephants, the great apes, and viverrid carnivores gives the impression of two very similar faunas, but there are also striking differences. The Oriental Region has no lemurs or their close kin, none of the numerous African antelope, or peculiarly African hystricomorph rodents such as cane rats, mole rats, and gundis. Four families—including tree shrews, "flying lemurs," tarsiers, and spiny dormice—are endemic.

The Palearctic Region is the largest in area. Its mostly temperate climate ranges from the hot deserts of North Africa and the Middle East to the severe cold of the Arctic tundra. The mammal fauna is diverse—40 families are represented—but only two families are endemic, the Spalacidae (mole rats) and the Seleviniidae (central Asian dormouse). About 78% of the families are shared with the Ethiopian Region and 70% with the

Oriental Region. Eurasia remained linked to North America by the Bering land bridge for part of the Tertiary, which facilitated migration of mammals in both directions. Today the two regions have many families, and even a few species, in common—Felidae (cats), Canidae (wolves and foxes), Soricidae (shrews), Muridae (voles), Ursidae (bears), Vespertilionidae (bats), Mustelidae (weasels), and Cervidae (deer).

The Nearctic Region is similar to the Palearctic. Here, too, glaciations in the Quaternary period had a decisive influence on the fauna, destroying much of what had existed before, and paving the way for a new fauna with a greater ability to adapt. Much of the mammal fauna is shared with the Neotropical Region (more than 75% of the families); only two families are endemic, the Aplodontidae (mountain beavers) and the Antilocapridae (pronghorn antelope).

The Neotropical Region consists largely of vast tropical rain forest in the lowlands, with highland cloud forests. Tropical savanna and grassland extend over southern South America and occur in patches in Central America. The extreme habitats of arid desert and high alpine tundra are found in both Central and South America. Although South America has been isolated through most of the geologic past since the Cretaceous, the Central American isthmus formed a land bridge late in the Pliocene, affording an interchange of fauna which persisted into modern times. The neotropics are rich in mammals, with 46 families represented. Twenty of these are endemic. Nonetheless, the Neotropical Region shares one-third of its families of mammals with the Palearctic, a sign of an ancient and active process of diffusion. Peculiar to the neotropics are cebid monkeys, all the edentates—anteaters, sloths, and armadillos—opossums, and certain hystricomorph rodents such as the capybara, cavy, chinchilla, and nutria or coypu. The Andean llama, alpaca, and vicuña are New World relatives of the camel. Tapirs are also found in both the Neotropical and Oriental Regions.

The Australian Region is unique. It has no land connection with any other faunal realm, and in fact is composed of an island continent—Australia proper—and several nearby, but isolated, islands. The northern part of the region, including extreme northern Australia, lies in the tropics and is covered by evergreen forest. The west and interior of Australia consist of vast arid land, much of it extreme desert, while the eastern and southeastern montane belt and Tasmania are temperate in climate, with eucalyptus forests and woodlands. The renowned Australian mammal fauna is likewise unique. It is the result of Australia's long isolation and the dramatic radiation of marsupials—the pouched mammals—during that time. Perhaps as far back as the Paleocene epoch marsupials first invaded Australia from their South American homeland via Antarctica, then a land bridge between the two regions. By the Eocene, Australia had broken away, become an island continent, and drifted northeast, carrying its marsupials with it. With no significant competition from placental mammals, the marsupials filled virtually all the ecological niches available, evolving into an array of forms unequaled in any other single order of mammals. Marsupials grew to superficially resemble their placental ecological counterparts of other regions. For example, the marsupial mole developed powerful and clawed front feet for burrowing; the predatory thylacine resembled the Holarctic wolf; gliders grew membranes between their limbs in imitation of "flying" squirrels; and so forth. The analogy, however, is not absolutely complete, for there are neither truly flying marsupials nor marine ones. Even in Australia these niches are occupied by true bats of many species, seals, whales, and dugongs. And these are not the only placental mammals inhabiting Australia. A number of rodents are also found there. Their ancestors probably arrived on floating debris from New Guinea. The dingo, a variety of domestic dog, was brought by man. The unique egg-laying mammals, the monotremes (the platypus and echidnas), are an order found only in the Australian Region.

CHARACTERISTICS OF MAMMALS

Mammals are complex organisms and share many features with other classes of animals with which they have a common origin. Two readily apparent features set mammals apart from any other living vertebrates: they nourish their young with milk secreted by special organs on the mother's body, known as mammary glands, and they have hair. Although it is the unique glands, or mammae, from which the name "mammal" is derived, the development of hair came first in the long evolutionary history of mammals.

Moving into unoccupied ecological niches was an advantage in the revolution of mammals. The development of hair in their reptilian ancestors made such adaptations possible, for hair and the unique sweat glands accompanying it allowed these small creatures to control their body temperature. They had become homeothermic, or warm-blooded. No longer dependent upon the warm daylight to rouse them from overnight torpor, these creatures with their newly acquired fur coats were now insulated against the cold and could maintain a more regular body temperature. This enabled them to feed at night and avoid reptilian predators, which were still active only by day. A muscular system developed that would allow mammals to raise or lower their body hairs, exposing the skin and thus regulating the insulatory effect of a fur coat. Seasonal changes——heavy coat for winter, light in summer——further enhanced the advantages of having hair.

The glands associated with hairs brought additional benefits. By secreting water from the bloodstream, sweat glands set up an evaporative cooling system. Sebaceous glands secrete oil to waterproof the hair. The modification of certain skin glands resulted in the mammary glands which allowed mammals to nourish their young directly. Such maternal care permits mammals to bear fewer offspring, yet enjoy a higher rate of survival. This efficient system was completed when mammals gave up laying eggs and were able to bear their young alive, nourished during fetal development. By maintaining a constant high temperature, mammals not only could become nocturnal in habit but could tolerate a variety of habitats. With these advances

came more active, efficient, and alert mammals. Higher energy required greater efficiency in both the circulatory and respiratory systems, together with a larger and more complex brain. Structural improvements evolved in the heart and blood vessels, which in turn supplied well-oxygenated blood to the brain, while the volume of oxygen breathed was increased by the development of a muscular diaphragm separating the thorax and abdomen. Thus the agile mammal added intelligence to the many advances over its reptilian ancestors.

But such improvements demanded enhancement. Speed and agility depend upon limbs placed more effectively under the animal's body to support its weight and thrust it forward. As mammals began to radiate into a greater variety of habitats, their limbs continued to adapt to new ways of life. Long, narrow legs developed, giving browsing ungulates access to the tender leaves of trees, and multiplying their speed to escape carnivorous predators. Small arboreal mammals, as flying squirrels, evolved strong membranes between their limbs permitting them to glide from tree to tree. Burrowing mammals (moles) formed massive shoulders, heavy forearms, and sharp claws for digging. Perhaps the most extreme cases are the elongated fingers with sheer membranes that form the wings of bats and the limbs modified into flippers for marine species such as whales.

Competition among mammals themselves led to even further evolution. The senses became sharper. An array of special devices also evolved by which mammals could protect themselves from predators. Enormous girth and thick skin serve to protect elephants, rhinos, and hippos, while armadillos hid within a hard shell. If you have ever encountered a porcupine or handled a hedgehog, you are familiar with their protective device—sharp quills. And who has not experienced the ready defense of a skunk? Often, however, such animals do not have to resort to spraying potential enemies because their bright, contrasting coloration acts as a warning signal. Many mammals, particularly grazing or browsing forms, have evolved a striped coat color, or a spotted pattern as in cats and some other carnivores, to conceal themselves in grass or among shrubs. Protective coloration is widespread among virtually all orders of mammals.

In addition to protective needs and adaptation to new environments, the feeding habits of mammals also produced anatomical changes. Among them were improvements in the digestive system to make it more efficient and able to extract sufficient energy from the food consumed. Paramount among the adaptations to feeding habits are mammals' teeth. Instead of the simple spiked form that serves reptiles, mammalian teeth have differentiated into biting or gnawing incisors; sharp, flesh-stabbing canines; chewing or grinding premolars and molars. Indeed, the dentition, because of its many minute differences, is used by scientists to classify the thousands of species of mammals that once inhabited this earth or do so today.

Skin and hair

Skin consists of two layers, the outer protective layer being the epidermis, made up of dead cells, and the layer beneath, the dermis, which is attached to the muscles of the body. Where covered with hair the epidermis is usually soft; otherwise it is thick—as in elephants—or even cornified, as in the foot pads of dogs. Nails, claws, and hooves, and the horns of sheep, cattle, and antelope, are likewise cornified structures that grow continuously from the base. Horns have an inner core of bone for support. The antlers of deer and their relatives, however, are annual growths—shed each year—consisting of tissue that becomes calcified.

Hair is composed of dead epidermal cells and the protein keratin. The color of a hair is determined by the pigment it contains, and a single hair can be of one or several colors. Collectively, the hairs or fur of a mammal, or pelage, consists of a fine undercoat for insulation; scattered guard hairs—long, coarse hairs that help protect the pelage from wear; and special sensory hairs, or vibrissae, commonly called whiskers. These are extremely important to the rodents and carnivores whose faces they decorate, for at the base of each vibrissa are nerves that make the hair a delicate sensing device to help the animal feel his way about. The pelage is thickest on mammals that inhabit cold and temperate climates; sparse and short on tropical species. Elephants, rhinos, and hippos have few hairs. Whales and dolphins bear hairs around the mouth, but otherwise make up for the absence of hair with heavy layers of insulating fat, or blubber, beneath the skin. There is a naked, or practically so, mole rat—a burrowing rodent in east Africa—

Hairs are typical of mammals, even though certain species have subsequently lost them as a result of adaptation to specific ways of life. Special muscles situated at the base of the hairs enable them to stand erect.

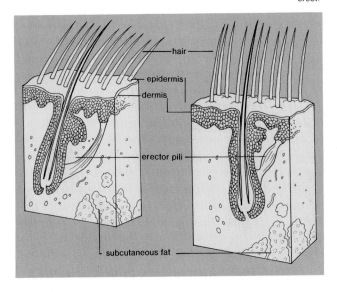

and there are two nearly unfurred species of bats.

Hair follicles are provided with sebaceous glands, which secrete an oily lubrication for the hairs and epidermis. Sweat glands in the skin help cool the body through evaporation and they eliminate wastes. The mammaries are modified sweat glands that secrete milk. In most mammals the mammary opens in a teat, or nipple, but the egg-laying monotremes have no such structure. Instead, the milk oozes from the glands and is sucked by the young from tufts of hair. The number of nipples on other mammals ranges from a single pair on the breast in bats and primates (including man), five or six pairs in some ungulates, to more in some rodents and marsupials, and a maximum of 11 pair in the tenrecs of Madagascar. They may extend from the breast to the abdomen or be concentrated in the female's abdominal area.

Bone structure

The hard parts of a mammal's body are the skeleton—a collection of some 200 bones—and it is the framework that supports the body. In the so-called lower animals, like lobsters or insects, an outer shell—the exoskeleton—holds the soft body together, but in mammals and all their cousins—fishes, amphibians, reptiles, and birds—the endoskeleton supports the body from within. Indeed, all such animals are known collectively as "vertebrates," or "backboned" animals, after part of this important feature. The skeleton is not simply a framework, however; it functions to protect the highly developed nervous

25

system and the digestive system from injury and to secure the muscles, which in turn move the bones that give the animal mobility and agility. In mammals the skeleton is simpler than that of reptiles through a greater fusion of bones. There is more actual strong, bony material than cartilage, permitting the more secure muscle attachment needed for the agility and greater speed of mammals. The skull together with the vertebral column and ribs form the axial skeleton; the limbs and the bones holding them are the appendicular skeleton.

The skull, or cranium, is made up of many bones fused together into a sort of box to house the brain. This braincase is large in mammals to accommodate the increased brain size over that of reptiles. The cranium provides a surface for attachment of the temporal muscles, which close the jaws. There is in many mammals, such as carnivores, a pronounced sagittal crest atop the cranium to permit firmer attachment of these strong muscles. The facial part of the skull forms the muzzle. It holds the upper teeth and protects the sense organs. The curved zygomatic arch, a bone structure dating back to the ancient mammal-like reptiles, forms the lower part of the eye socket and also articulates with the mandible, or lower jaw. On each side of the cranium are the tiny bones of the middle and inner ears; in many species the tympanic bone over the middle ear is enlarged and shaped like a round box, called the tympanic bulla. At the extreme rear of the cranium is a large opening, the foramen magnum, through which the spinal nerve cord is connected to the brain. On each side of this is the joint on

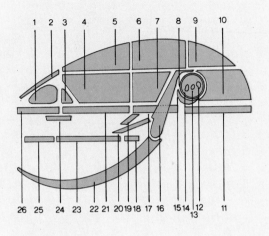

Left: *in albino specimens, like this young gorilla, there is a total absence of pigment. The skin is pink, the hair white, and the eyes red. Below: a diagram of the cranial bones: 1. turbinaa; 2. nasal; 3. lacrimal; 4. orbitosphenoid; 5. frontal; 6. parietal; 7. alisphenoid; 8. petrosal; 9. supraoccipital; 10. exoccipital; 11. basioccipital; 12. stapes, or stirrup bone; 13. incus; 14. malleus; 15. ectotympanic; 16. squamosal; 17. basisphenoid; 18. palatine; 19. pterygoid; 20. jugal, or maiar; 21. presphenoid; 22. dentary; 23. maxillary; 24. vomer; 25. premaxillary; 26. mesethmoid.*

which the skull pivots on the first vertebra, or atlas. The fact that there are two such joints (one on either side of the skull) and the way the neck muscles are attached prevent the head from swiveling completely around.

The spinal column is composed of vertebrae which are jointed with each other by flexible discs, affording freedom of movement. The spinal cord passes through the center of the cylindrical vertebrae and is thus protected. Nearly all mammals have seven neck, or cervical, vertebrae, be they giraffes, mice, or men. The manatee and two-toed sloth have six, pangolins sometimes have eight, and the three-toed sloth has nine. The caudal vertebrae are tapered to form the tail, and in apes and man the four rudimentary bones are reduced to form the coccyx. The rib cage, attached to the thoracic portion of the spine and joined at the breastbone, protects the heart and lungs.

Except in highly modified marine forms—whales and sea cows—mammals have four limbs. The pectoral girdle—shoulder blade and collarbones—supports the forelimbs, and the pelvic girdle fixes the hind limbs to the axial skeleton. The upper-arm bone is the humerus; the corresponding upper-leg bone, the femur. These are followed by a pair of bones side by side—the radius in the forearm, the tibia and fibula in the shin, or lower leg. A variety of bones follow to form the carpals of the wrist and tarsals of the ankle, jointed with which, in turn, are metacarpals, or hand bones, and metatarsals, or foot bones. Fingers and toes are made up of phalanges. The length, shape, even number of these bones vary widely due to the re-

The bone structure of the foot has evolved into (1) the digitigrade mode of stealthy carnivores, (2) the plantigrade form, a basic posture for walking, and (3) the unguligrade, or hoofed type, for fast running.

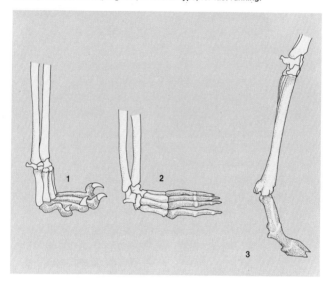

markable adaptive radiation of mammals in all types of habitats, where their way of life demands quite specific types of limbs. Compare, for example, the lumbering rhinoceros, darting chipmunk, swinging gibbon, burrowing mole, flying bat, racing cheetah, and jumping kangaroo. Those mammals that walk by placing the entire sole and heel on the ground are called plantigrade, and include man and bears. We distinguish as digitigrade animals such as dogs and cats that walk on the undersurface of the digits, or toes. And horses, having evolved from five-toed through four- and three-toed ancestors, now walk on just a single toe or hoof on each foot; they are termed unguligrade.

Teeth

Nearly all mammals have teeth, although in the baleen whales they are absent or present only in the fetal stage and do not appear above the gums. An example of convergent evolution (that is, unrelated animals in the same ecological niche acquiring similar adaptive features) can be seen in African and Asian pangolins, true anteaters of the neotropics, and egg-laying echidnas of Australia and New Guinea. None of these unrelated creatures (aside from being mammals) has any teeth; they are all highly specialized ant or termite eaters.

Teeth vary according to their function and position. The usually small front teeth, incisors, bite or gnaw and are particularly prominent in rodents—beavers, especially—and in elephants the uppers are tusks. The eyeteeth, or canines, are the

Skulls and dentition of certain mammals: 1. aardvark (*Tubulidentata*); 2. bear (*Carnivora*); 3. bat (*Chiroptera*); 4. horse (*Perissodactyla*); 5. hare (*Lagomorpha*); 6. pocket gopher (*Rodentia*) (vertical section); 7. rat (*Rodentia*); 8. monkey (*Primates*).

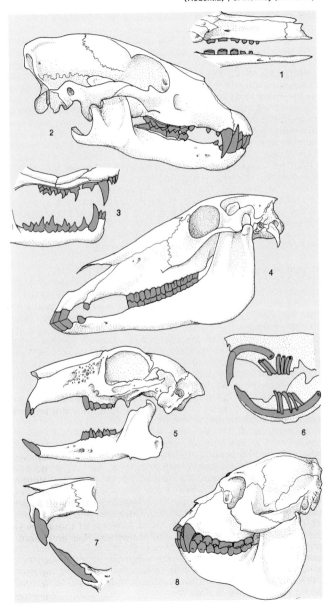

pointed, stabbing teeth adjacent to the incisors. They are most conspicuous in carnivores and in fact derive their name from dogs. They form the tusks of pigs. The canine teeth are used for tearing and for seizing prey. The cheek teeth, premolars and molars, are wider, with complex crowns, and are used for crushing and grinding.

During its lifetime a mammal will usually have two sets of teeth. The deciduous, or milk, teeth are shed as the animal grows, being replaced by the permanent set. Molars are not found among milk teeth. The incisors of rodents and molars of some herbivores are put to hard use and therefore continue to grow as the outer ends wear away.

While some marsupials have as many as 50 teeth and long-beaked dolphins may have up to 260 simplified teeth, as a rule the complete dentition in mammals does not exceed 44. The number and type of teeth, important diagnostic characters in classification, are expressed in a dental formula for each species. The number of each type of tooth in the upper jaw is written over the corresponding number for the lower jaw; for example, in the pig there are incisors 3/3, canines 1/1, premolars 4/4, molars 3/3. Since this applies only to one side of the jaw, the total is multiplied by 2 to arrive at the complete complement of teeth—in this case 22 × 2, or 44. The order is always the same and can be abbreviated, as in this dental formula for man: 2/2, 1/1, 3/3, 2/2 × 2 = 32.

Digestive system

Digestion of food begins in the mouth and is completed in the intestine. The premolars and molars break up the food in the mouth, where saliva begins to digest any starch and wets the fragmented food for easier swallowing. The food then passes through the gullet, in the chest cavity, and into the stomach, just beyond the diaphragm. Gastric juices in the stomach break the food down, but except for alcohol, it is not absorbed there. Some mammals have a compartmentalized stomach, especially well developed in ruminants as cattle, deer, and camels. In their case the huge bulk of herbage consumed is largely cellulose, which cannot be digested by any natural enzyme known in the animal's body. It therefore first passes into the rumen, where there are bacteria and protozoa that break down the cellulose. A soft, fermented cud then returns to the animal's mouth for continued chewing, or ruminating, then on to a second stomach compartment, the reticulum. The food passes in turn to two additional compartments, the omasum and abomasum, for further digestion. In all mammals the partly digested food leaves the stomach to enter the duodenum, where enzymes from the pancreas and bile from the liver via the gallbladder are added. Digestion and ultimate absorption of nutrients into the blood takes place in the long small intestine; the remaining matter passes into the relatively short colon, or large intestine, from which it is finally excreted. Many nonruminating herbivorous mammals, rodents in particular, have an appendage—the caecum—extending out from between the small and large intestines, in which bacteria break down the cellulose in their food.

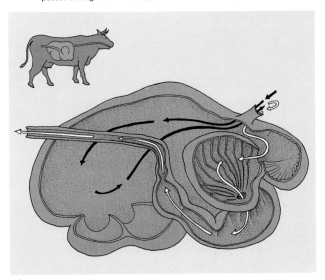

Circulation and respiration

The nutrients absorbed into the bloodstream after digestion are circulated throughout the body via a highly efficient circulatory system. The heart in mammals, as in birds and some reptiles, is divided into four chambers—two auricles and two ventricles—whose muscular walls regularly contract to pump the blood. Refreshed blood is sent from the left ventricle through the aorta, the main artery, which branches into smaller arteries and finally tiny capillaries, thus circulating blood to all the cells of the body. Here the blood exchanges oxygen for waste gas—carbon dioxide; it then flows toward the heart through the veins and ultimately through the large vena cava, passing into the right auricle. The veins and heart are provided with valves to keep the blood flowing in the proper direction. The gas-laden blood journeys from the right auricle to the right ventricle, then goes directly to the spongelike lungs, where it now exchanges carbon dioxide for fresh oxygen. The newly oxygenated blood is then returned to the left auricle of the heart, flows into the left ventricle, and is once again pumped through the body. The rate at which the heart contracts, or beats, varies widely among diverse mammals; it can be as slow as 20 beats per minute in gigantic whales, or more than 1,300 beats per minute in a tiny shrew.

The heart and lungs together fill the chest cavity. When a breath is taken, the air passes down the trachea and into the paired bronchi, which branch into small passages, or bronchioles, that in turn spread into small alveolar ducts. The

31

The uterus, or womb, takes on various configurations in mammals: (1) double with an outlet shared with the intestine in monotremes; (2) double with two vaginas in marsupials; (3) bifid, or forked, in rodents; (4) two-pronged in carnivores and ungulates (5) single in the primates and bats.

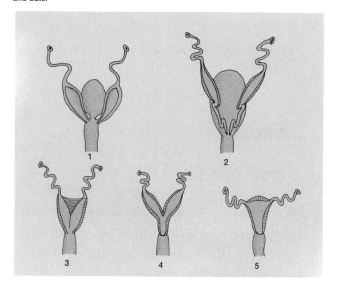

lungs, two porous masses side by side, consist of countless minute chambers, or alveoli, through whose membranes inhaled air is exchanged with the carbon dioxide waste in the blood. There are some 300 million alveoli in a human lung, collectively totaling more than 600 square feet of surface area for respiration. When you take a breath, it is the muscular expansion of the thorax which forces the lungs to inhale as the air pressure is reduced in an enlarged, sealed compartment, creating a partial vacuum. Although the muscles pulling the ribs outward help in each such expansion, it is the diaphragm which is really responsible for every breath taken. This muscle, a sophisticated development found only in mammals, seals off the thoracic cavity from the abdomen; when it contracts, it stretches backward (downward in man) into the abdomen, thereby expanding the chest for each new breath.

Reproduction

Animals must reproduce to ensure continuation of the species. In simple invertebrates this is merely a matter of the single-celled animal's dividing itself in two; in some others a new organism grows from the body of its parent and breaks off. By the time we reach mammals, however, the matter has become much more complex. Fundamentally, as in all other vertebrates, cells from two different individuals—an egg cell from the female and a sperm cell from a male—are united to grow and form a new individual. By reason of having two parents, the young is not an identical duplicate of another individual but

In some species the young can stand and walk immediately after birth, while others are quite helpless and immobile. It is at the moment of birth that the risk of predation is most critical for both mother and young.

instead is a genetic combination of two, thus providing a greater potential for evolutionary advance. As in reptiles and birds, fertilization in mammals is internal.

Transfer of male sperm to the body of the female is made through the penis, the male copulatory organ. It is composed of erectile tissue and in many mammals, but not man, contains a bone known as the baculum. Sperm cells are produced in the paired testes which usually are situated together in the scrotum, a saclike appendage that serves to keep the testes at a cooler temperature than inside the body. The sperm pass during coitus through small tubes into the urethra, the connecting tube that runs through the penis and is also used for urination. In the female, the paired ovaries are situated in the pelvis and contain thousands of eggs, or ova. As each egg matures, it is released through the oviduct, or fallopian tube, through which it passes into the uterus for fertilization and subsequent development. The uterus opens into the vagina, the passage through which the male penis enters. There are two vaginas and two uteri in monotremes and marsupials. In placental mammals there is but one vagina; the uteri, however, are separate in rodents and incompletely fused in insectivores, carnivores, and ungulates. Primates have a single uterus.

Monotremes are oviparous, or egg-laying, mammals. Marsupials are ovoviviparous, which means the egg is large and has a yolk adequate to nourish the embryo during its early development, but it remains unattached to the wall of the uterus. Gestation in marsupials is necessarily short, therefore, and the young are born in an immature, fetal stage. They make their way to the mother's pouch and continue to grow, nourished with milk. All other mammals, termed placental, are viviparous. Their small egg, lacking food substance, becomes attached to the uterine wall, and the developing embryo is nourished by the mother's blood passing through a placenta. This process allows longer gestation, and as a result the young are born in a more advanced state of development.

The reproductive cycles vary considerably among placental mammals, depending upon the length of gestation. In elephants the gestation period is as long as 22 months, although size alone is not the determining factor; the giant among all mammals, the blue whale, has a gestation period of only 11 months. Many bats and certain other mammals have a delayed implantation in which the fertilized ovum remains dormant or its development is retarded at first, thus considerably extending the gestation period and delaying birth until the optimal season of warm weather or abundant food. Thus the gestation period of the fisher, a small North American carnivore with delayed implantation, is 48 to 51 weeks, or about the same as that of the blue whale. The length of gestation varies from 22 to 45 days in squirrels, 2 to 7 months in New World porcupines, 6 months in bears, 14 to 15 months in giraffes.

Animals having long gestation periods or whose young mature slowly and are suckled for a long time do not breed as often as others. Some mice often breed throughout spring, summer, and autumn; have a gestation period of three weeks; and the females can breed at 21 days of age. Many mammals, as beavers, coyotes, and weasels, breed once a year. Many other species, however, are able to breed twice each year, and even three times in one year is not uncommon. Environmental conditions to which various species have adapted play a role in their breeding cycles. It is advantageous for the young to be born during the season of least severe weather and to be weaned when food is most abundant. Many tropical mammals breed throughout the year and young are born accordingly. In temperate and cold climates, the young are most often born in spring or summer.

Similar factors also influence the number of young born among different species. Their rate of growth until weaned, mortality rates, the adult activity cycles, and other factors no doubt help determine the litter size as well. Many rodents have three to six young per litter; a few species of mice can have as many as eighteen. Seals, whales, and most species of primates and bats bear only a single young at one time.

The senses

The sense of smell is not the same in all mammals. It is highly developed in some insectivores, whose olfactory lobes of the brain are proportionately large. They are also prominent in carnivores and rodents, but poorly developed in whales and higher primates. Our sense of smell as humans is obviously no match for that of our dogs. Porpoises and dolphins have no olfactory system. In other mammals, the olfactory nerves (which sense odors) are located on a moist mucous membrane over a